THE TRY NOT TO LAUGH CHALLENGE

WOULD YOU RATHER?

CHRISTMAS Edition

Try Not To Laugh Challenge
BONUS PLAY

Join our Joke Club and get the Bonus Play PDF!

Simply send us an email to:

TNTLPublishing@gmail.com

and you will get the following:

- 10 Hilarious Would You Rather Questions
- An entry in our Monthly Giveaway of a $50 Amazon Gift card!

We draw a new winner each month and will contact you via email!

Good luck!

Welcome to
The Try Not to Laugh Challenge
Would You Rather?
CHRISTMAS EDITION

RULES:

- Face your opponent and decide who is 'Elf 1' and 'Elf 2'.

- Starting with 'Elf 1', read the Would You Rather question aloud and pick an answer. The same player will then explain why they chose that answer in the most hilarious or wacky way possible!

- If the reason makes 'Elf 2' laugh, then a laugh point is scored!

- Take turns going back and forth, then mark your total laugh points at the end of each round!

- Whoever gets the most laugh points is officially crowned the 'Laugh Master'!

- If ending with a tie, finish with the Tie-Breaker round for WINNER TAKES ALL!

Most importantly, have fun and be SILLY! 

REMEMBER, the scenarios found in this book are solely for fun and games! Please do NOT attempt any of the crazy scenarios in this book.

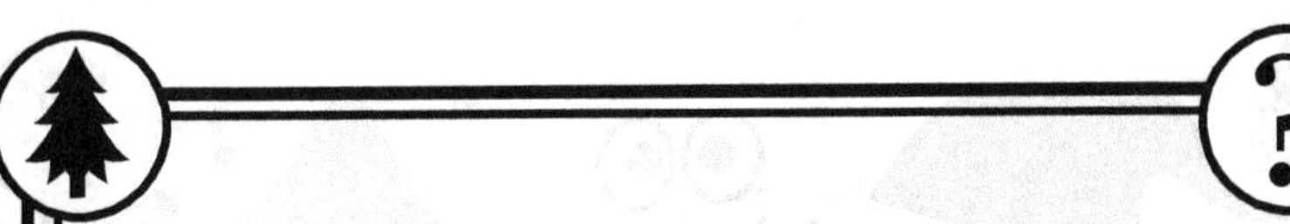
ROUND

1

ELF 1

(DON'T FORGET TO EXPLAIN YOUR ANSWERS!)

Would you rather see nothing but flashing holiday lights every time you close your eyes, OR have to fight off a flock of smelly emperor penguins, using only a broken candy cane?

Laugh Point____ /1

Would you rather wear a hat made from reindeer fur OR a scarf made from Christmas lights?

Laugh Point____ /1

ELF 1

(DON'T FORGET TO EXPLAIN YOUR ANSWERS!)

Would you rather write 5 Christmas carols and sing them to your neighbors, OR recite an original Christmas poem on the local news channel?

Laugh Point____/1

Would you rather give 100 Christmas cards to strangers OR sing carols on the side of the road for an hour?

Laugh Point____/1

Pass the book to ELF 2! →

ELF 2

(DON'T FORGET TO EXPLAIN YOUR ANSWERS!)

Would you rather have a pizza topped with turkey and mashed potatoes, OR have turkey and mashed potatoes topped with cheese and pepperoni for Christmas dinner?

Laugh Point____/1

Would you rather make a life-size gingerbread house OR a life-size gingerbread man cookie?

Laugh Point____/1

ELF 2

(DON'T FORGET TO EXPLAIN YOUR ANSWERS!)

Would you rather drink a gallon of hot cocoa within 30 minutes OR a gallon of eggnog in 10 minutes?

Laugh Point____/1

Would you rather have a snowman come to life like Frosty and spend all day with him, OR meet Santa Claus on Christmas Eve, but never remember?

Laugh Point____/1

SCORE BOARD

Add up each Elf's laugh points for this round!

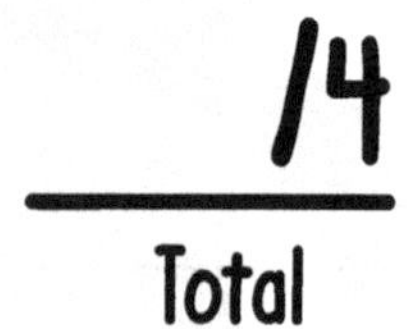

ELF 1

/4

Total

ELF 2

____

ROUND CHAMPION

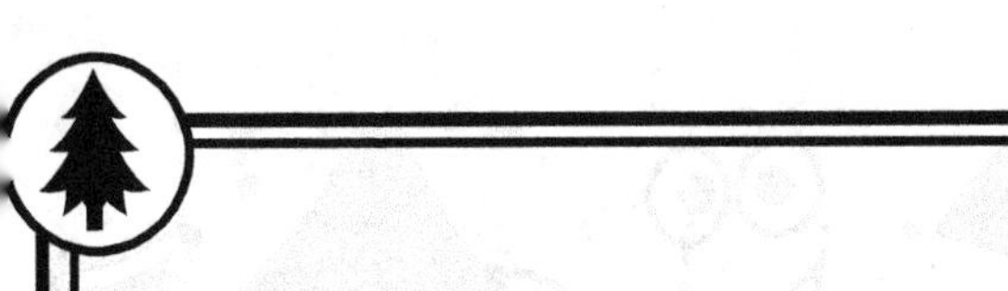

ROUND

2

ELF 1

(DON'T FORGET TO EXPLAIN YOUR ANSWERS!)

Would you rather your presents be wrapped in sticky, gluey paper OR be required to determine a secret code to unlock and open each one?

Laugh Point____/1

Would you rather lose your ability to see the colors green and red, but still see all other colors OR only be able to see green and red?

Laugh Point____/1

ELF 1

(DON'T FORGET TO EXPLAIN YOUR ANSWERS!)

Would you rather be Santa's workshop photographer and take 100 pictures of kids with Santa, OR have to read 100 Christmas lists from kids to Santa?

Laugh Point____/1

Would you rather spend a full day making 20 snow angels outside OR making 50 cups of hot cocoa and marshmallows, inside?

Laugh Point____/1

Pass the book to ELF 2! →

ELF 2

(DON'T FORGET TO EXPLAIN YOUR ANSWERS!)

Would you rather become a great ice-hockey player, but every now and then suddenly turn into a pile of snow, OR be the best in the world at throwing snowballs, but have to wear mittens made out of old ham?

Laugh Point____/1

Would you rather wear an ugly Christmas sweater OR elf ears for a week?

Laugh Point____/1

ELF 2

(DON'T FORGET TO EXPLAIN YOUR ANSWERS!)

Would you rather catch all the melting water droplets from a melting igloo, using only pots and pans OR try to ski down a mountain, standing on frozen sausages?

Laugh Point____/1

Would you rather get nothing, but ugly sweaters for Christmas, OR a video game that would break in 24 hours?

Laugh Point____/1

SCORE BOARD

Add up each Elf's laugh points for this round!

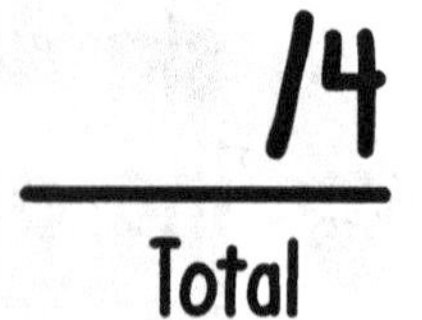

/4

Total

ELF 1

/4

Total

ELF 2

____

ROUND CHAMPION

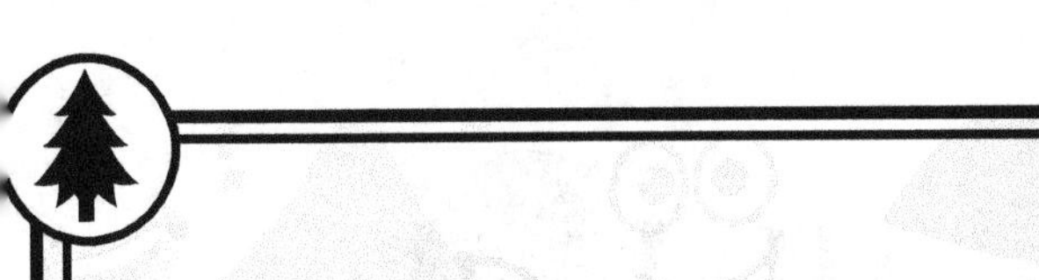

ROUND

ELF 1

(DON'T FORGET TO EXPLAIN YOUR ANSWERS!)

Would you rather eat an entire loaf of fruitcake without anything to wash it down, OR drink a milkshake made with black olives?

Laugh Point____/1

Would you rather get into a snowball fight with Christmas cookie-flavored snow cones OR chocolate fudge ice cream?

Laugh Point____/1

ELF 1

(DON'T FORGET TO EXPLAIN YOUR ANSWERS!)

Would you rather open all of your presents on Christmas Eve OR have to hunt for them on Christmas morning like Easter Eggs?

Laugh Point_____/1

Would you rather put up a fake, plastic Christmas tree that smells like dirty laundry OR put up a live tree that has a family of birds, who never stop singing in it?

Laugh Point_____/1

Pass the book to ELF 2! →

ELF 2

(DON'T FORGET TO EXPLAIN YOUR ANSWERS!)

Would you rather be an elf in Santa's workshop screwing wheels onto toy cars all day, OR eat ten pounds of old frozen carrots that used to be snowman noses?

Laugh Point____/1

Would you rather grow a giant white Santa beard and have to start every sentence with "Ho, Ho, Ho!" OR have your ears replaced by pine cones?

Laugh Point____/1

(DON'T FORGET TO EXPLAIN YOUR ANSWERS!)

Would you rather be forced to listen to 'Let It Go' on repeat for 3 days, OR spend 24 hours singing 'Jingle Bells' non-stop?

Laugh Point____/1

Would you rather decorate a 100-foot Christmas tree OR take down Christmas lights off of 3 houses?

Laugh Point____/1

SCORE BOARD

Add up each Elf's laugh points for this round!

ELF 1

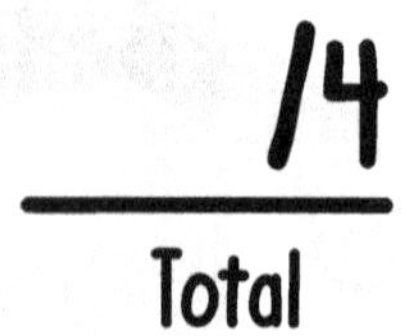

/4

Total

ELF 2

____

ROUND CHAMPION

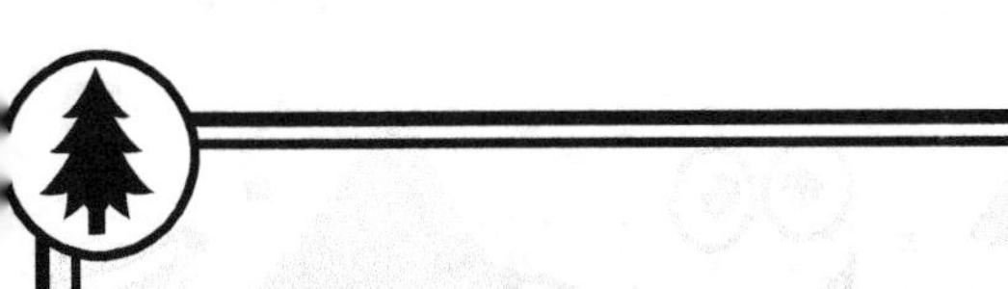

ROUND

ELF 1

(DON'T FORGET TO EXPLAIN YOUR ANSWERS!)

Would you rather have to write all the thank-you notes for your entire family using pink ink, OR spend the night stuck in a chimney with Santa Claus, after you both ate beans for dinner?

Laugh Point____/1

Would you rather grow your own Christmas tree OR have to make each ornament by hand?

Laugh Point____/1

ELF 1

(DON'T FORGET TO EXPLAIN YOUR ANSWERS!)

Would you rather get to school by riding on the back of a giant polar bear, OR fly there on a magic snowboard that stays in the air, as long as you don't blink?

Laugh Point____ /1

Would you rather have an unlimited supply of Christmas cookies OR candy?

Laugh Point____ /1

Pass the book to ELF 2! →

ELF 2

(DON'T FORGET TO EXPLAIN YOUR ANSWERS!)

Would you rather be an elf that lives in a workshop making presents OR an elf that lives in a tree making cookies?

Laugh Point____/1

Would you rather get worms in your stocking OR find a roach in your hot cocoa?

Laugh Point____/1

ELF 2

(DON'T FORGET TO EXPLAIN YOUR ANSWERS!)

Would you rather go to school wearing little green slippers with bells on the ends of the toes, OR have to sleep sitting up in a chair because itchy antlers have grown out of the top of your head?

Laugh Point____/1

Would you rather work for Santa all winter by picking up reindeer poop, OR mining coal to get eyes for snowmen?

Laugh Point____/1

SCORE BOARD

Add up each Elf's laugh points for this round!

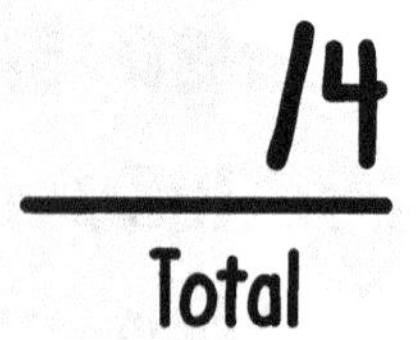

ELF 1

/4

Total

ELF 2

____

ROUND CHAMPION

ROUND 5

ELF 1

(DON'T FORGET TO EXPLAIN YOUR ANSWERS!)

Would you rather only wear elf slippers for the entire summer OR wear nothing but elf caps all spring?

Laugh Point____/1

Would you rather hug a baby reindeer OR be able to swim with a penguin family?

Laugh Point____/1

(DON'T FORGET TO EXPLAIN YOUR ANSWERS!)

Would you rather ride with Batman in his Batmobile OR ride with Santa in his sleigh?

Laugh Point____/1

Would you rather have one Christmas carol stuck in your head all year, OR have to walk around all year with your pants full of pine needles?

Laugh Point____/1

Pass the book to ELF 2! →

ELF 2

(DON'T FORGET TO EXPLAIN YOUR ANSWERS!)

Would you rather get snowed in for 2 weeks OR watch nothing but Christmas movies for 2 months?

Laugh Point____/1

Would you rather be best friends with Buddy the Elf OR Rudolph the Reindeer?

Laugh Point____/1

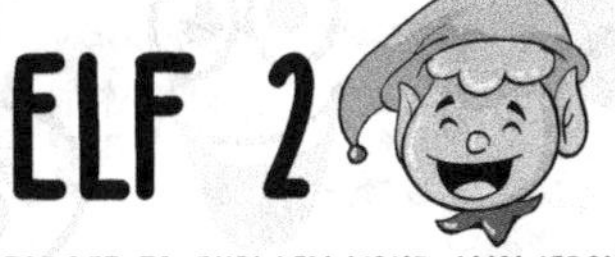

ELF 2

(DON'T FORGET TO EXPLAIN YOUR ANSWERS!)

Would you rather spend all winter wearing clothes made of wrapping paper, OR have to walk around with a pink ornament hanging off the tip of your nose?

Laugh Point____/1

Would you rather pretend to be a plastic elf in the front yard all night, OR sit in a bathtub of cold eggnog all day?

Laugh Point____/1

SCORE BOARD

Add up each Elf's laugh points for this round!

ELF 1

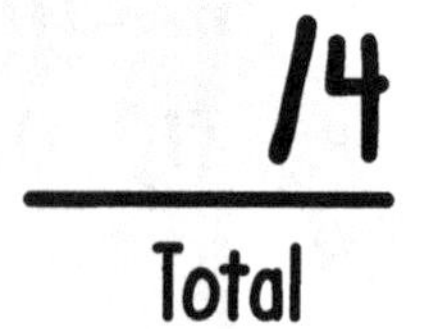

ELF 2

/4

Total

____

ROUND CHAMPION

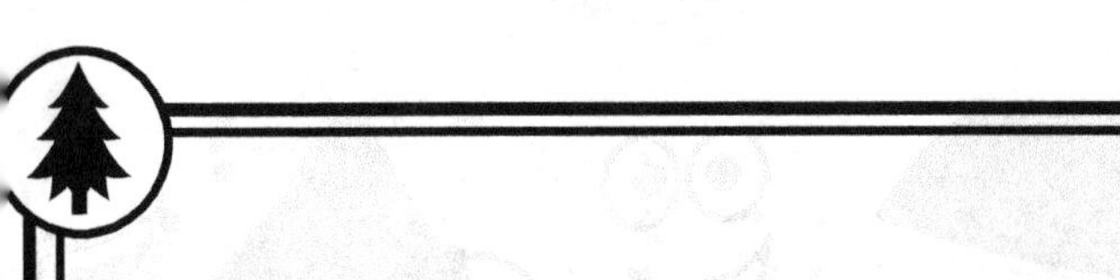
ROUND

6

ELF 1

(DON'T FORGET TO EXPLAIN YOUR ANSWERS!)

Would you rather go sledding with a polar bear OR ice skating with a penguin?

Laugh Point____/1

Would you rather not eat any sweet food for a year, OR have all the hair on your head turn into green tinsel?

Laugh Point____/1

(DON'T FORGET TO EXPLAIN YOUR ANSWERS!)

Would you rather be woken up every morning by a pumpkin pie falling on your face, OR go to bed each night wearing earmuffs made out of sea urchins?

Laugh Point____/1

Would you rather spend the last day of the year sledding with your favorite movie star OR be the star of a music video with dancing snowmen?

Laugh Point____/1

Pass the book to ELF 2! →

ELF 2

(DON'T FORGET TO EXPLAIN YOUR ANSWERS!)

Would you rather sleep in a cave with an angry skunk for a week OR be turned into a gingerbread man, balancing all night on a tightrope, over a lake of milk?

Laugh Point____/1

Would you rather open presents in slow motion, OR wait until after dinner to open gifts on Christmas?

Laugh Point____/1

ELF 2

(DON'T FORGET TO EXPLAIN YOUR ANSWERS!)

Would you rather drink whatever you want, but have to coat everything you eat with powdered cinnamon, OR eat whatever you want, but have nothing to drink except ice cold glacier water?

Laugh Point____ /1

Would you rather write a letter to Santa OR meet the Grinch?

Laugh Point____ /1

SCORE BOARD

Add up each Elf's laugh points for this round!

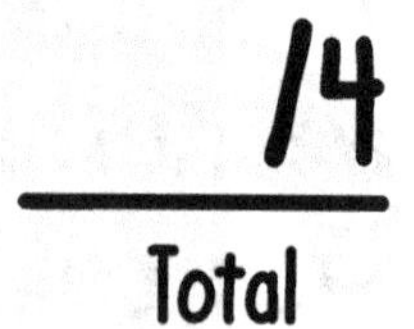

ELF 1

/4

Total

ELF 2

____

ROUND CHAMPION

ROUND
7

ELF 1

(DON'T FORGET TO EXPLAIN YOUR ANSWERS!)

Would you rather wrap yourself in 15 scarves to stay warm OR wear 12 pairs of socks at the same time?

Laugh Point____/1

Would you rather only drink eggnog, but eat whatever you would like for a week OR only eat candy canes, but be able to drink anything?

Laugh Point____/1

(DON'T FORGET TO EXPLAIN YOUR ANSWERS!)

Would you rather help Santa deliver presents, but be unable to leave the sleigh OR be able to drive his sleigh for 5 minutes, but have to wash it once he returns?

Laugh Point____/1

Would you rather decorate yourself like a walking Christmas tree OR wear a red scuba suit and Santa's beard?

Laugh Point____/1

Pass the book to ELF 2! →

ELF 2

(DON'T FORGET TO EXPLAIN YOUR ANSWERS!)

Would you rather have to walk through knee-deep snow that's like mashed potatoes all winter, OR be able to wear snowshoes that make it easy to walk, but you can't take them off (even in the shower)?

Laugh Point____/1

Would you rather be able to control who is on the naughty list OR the nice list?

Laugh Point____/1

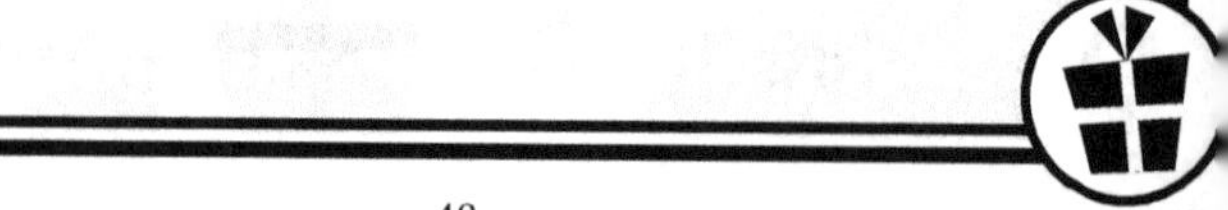

(DON'T FORGET TO EXPLAIN YOUR ANSWERS!)

Would you rather leave out spicy cookies and milk for Santa OR sweet cookies and sour milk?

Laugh Point____/1

Would you rather compete in a Christmas pie-eating contest OR in a Christmas hot cocoa drinking contest?

Laugh Point____/1

SCORE BOARD

Add up each Elf's laugh points for this round!

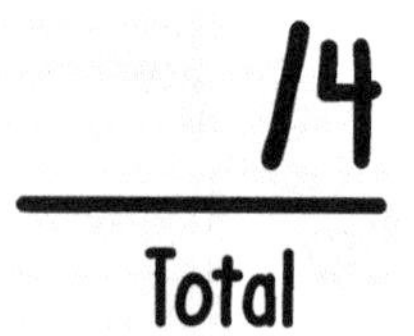

ELF 1

/4

Total

ELF 2

____

ROUND CHAMPION

ROUND
8

ELF 1

(DON'T FORGET TO EXPLAIN YOUR ANSWERS!)

Would you rather eat as many s'mores as you want, but have to wear a prickly plastic wreath around your neck, OR stay up as late as you want, but have to eat a pound of driveway salt that all your neighbors have walked on?

Laugh Point____/1

Would you rather be stuck inside of a snowglobe OR stuck in a Christmas tree?

Laugh Point____/1

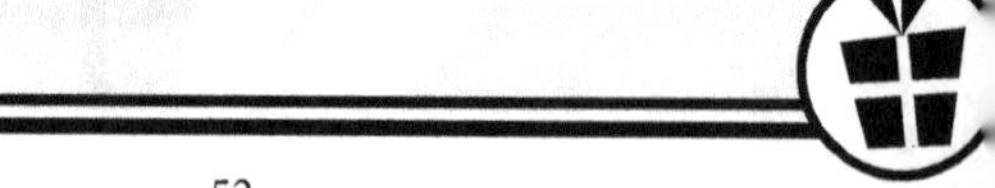

(DON'T FORGET TO EXPLAIN YOUR ANSWERS!)

Would you rather take a reindeer-pulled sleigh OR the Polar Express on your journey to the North Pole?

Laugh Point____ /1

Would you rather have the song 'Jingle Bells' OR 'Frosty the Snowman' stuck in your head for a week?

Laugh Point____ /1

Pass the book to ELF 2! →

ELF 2

(DON'T FORGET TO EXPLAIN YOUR ANSWERS!)

Would you rather have to enter every building through the chimney, OR yell "HO, HO, HO!" whenever you walked inside?

Laugh Point____/1

Would you rather have to hop everywhere you go because your feet are tied together with string lights, OR jump onto a snowdrift that may be full of broken lawn gnomes?

Laugh Point____/1

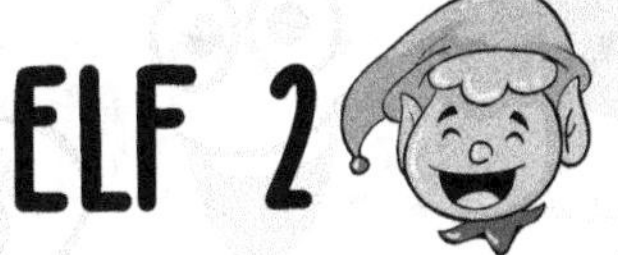

ELF 2

(DON'T FORGET TO EXPLAIN YOUR ANSWERS!)

Would you rather get an endless supply of hot chocolate, but have to shovel snow all day using only a shoe OR lie in bed watching all the TV you want, but have to eat a grapefruit-sized ball of old polar bear fur?

Laugh Point____/1

Would you rather have candy cane fingers OR a gumdrop nose?

Laugh Point____/1

SCORE BOARD

Add up each Elf's laugh points for this round!

ELF 1

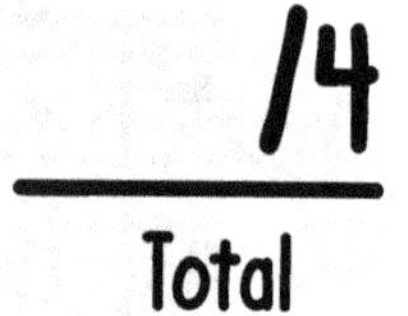

/4

Total

ELF 2

/4

Total

ROUND CHAMPION

ROUND
9

(DON'T FORGET TO EXPLAIN YOUR ANSWERS!)

Would you rather sleep in snow skis for a week OR wear a Santa suit you could never wash?

Laugh Point____/1

Would you rather have Christmas twice a year OR wake up to full stockings every other month?

Laugh Point____/1

(DON'T FORGET TO EXPLAIN YOUR ANSWERS!)

Would you rather be blasted in the face by a snow blower for an hour, OR have one of Grandma's fruitcakes fall on your head?

Laugh Point____/1

Would you rather have to hear Christmas music all day for a month, OR eat a three pound scented candle that tastes like reindeer sweat?

Laugh Point____/1

Pass the book to ELF 2! →

ELF 2

(DON'T FORGET TO EXPLAIN YOUR ANSWERS!)

Would you rather be able to move snow with the power of your mind, but have icicles grow out the ends of your fingers, OR have elves do all your homework, but be kept up at night because their village is under your bed?

Laugh Point____/1

Would you rather get buried in an avalanche OR spend a week in the Arctic, wearing a wet swimsuit?

Laugh Point____/1

ELF 2

(DON'T FORGET TO EXPLAIN YOUR ANSWERS!)

Would you rather live in a giant gingerbread house OR a mansion made out of fruitcakes?

Laugh Point____/1

Would you rather only get underwear for Christmas this year OR have to knit socks for your whole family?

Laugh Point____/1

SCORE BOARD

Add up each Elf's laugh points for this round!

ELF 1

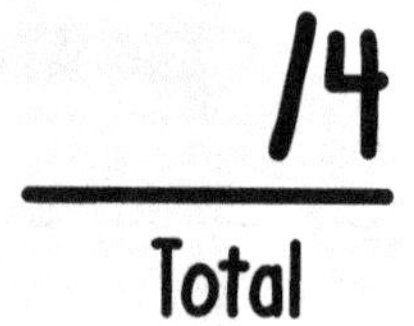

/4

____

Total

ELF 2

____

ROUND CHAMPION

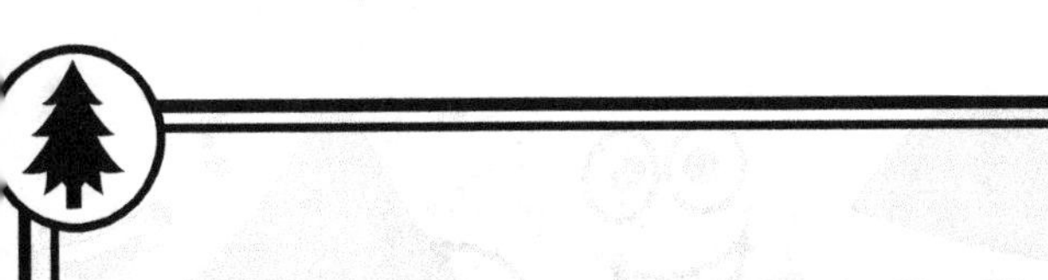

ROUND

(DON'T FORGET TO EXPLAIN YOUR ANSWERS!)

Would you rather decorate cookies with live spiders OR make fresh snot cider?

Laugh Point____/1

Would you rather clean Santa's workshop OR clean the reindeer stables?

Laugh Point____/1

(DON'T FORGET TO EXPLAIN YOUR ANSWERS!)

Would you rather be in a contest to see who can make the most snowmen in 30 minutes, OR who can make the most snow angels in 15 minutes?

Laugh Point____ /1

Would you rather catch the tooth fairy and keep all the money she hasn't left under pillows yet, OR catch Santa and keep all the presents?

Laugh Point____ /1

Pass the book to ELF 2! →

ELF 2

(DON'T FORGET TO EXPLAIN YOUR ANSWERS!)

Would you rather live in a gingerbread house OR an igloo?

Laugh Point____/1

Would you rather win seven gold medals in the Winter Olympics, but forget after a year that it ever happened, OR win one gold medal and remember it perfectly?

Laugh Point____/1

ELF 2

(DON'T FORGET TO EXPLAIN YOUR ANSWERS!)

Would you rather be a professional snowball thrower OR an award-winning snowman builder?

Laugh Point____/1

Would you rather paint yourself head to toe in green and red paint OR go to school in a Santa suit?

Laugh Point____/1

SCORE BOARD

Add up each Elf's laugh points for this round!

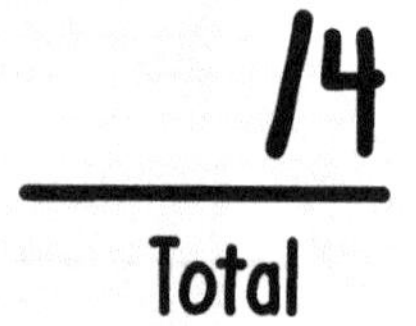

ELF 1

/4

Total

ELF 2

ROUND CHAMPION

Add up all your points from each round. The Elf with the most points is crowned

The Laugh Master!

In the event of a tie, continue to Round 11 - The Tie-Breaker Round!

ELF 1

Grand Total

ELF 2

Grand Total

THE LAUGH MASTER

ROUND 11

TIE-BREAKER

(WINNER TAKES ALL!)

ELF 1

(DON'T FORGET TO EXPLAIN YOUR ANSWERS!)

Would you rather go ice skating on a frozen pond made of hot cocoa, OR go downhill skiing on a big, marshmallow-covered mountain?

Laugh Point____/1

Would you rather have a speed tree-decorating contest OR who can decorate the tree best, while blindfolded contest?

Laugh Point____/1

(DON'T FORGET TO EXPLAIN YOUR ANSWERS!)

Would you rather put marshmallows OR peppermint on your turkey?

Laugh Point____/1

Would you rather sled with snowdogs OR dance with penguins?

Laugh Point____/1

Pass the book to ELF 2! →

(DON'T FORGET TO EXPLAIN YOUR ANSWERS!)

Would you rather have a stocking full of coal OR a gift made of ice?

Laugh Point____/1

Would you rather be a Jack-in-the-Box OR a Nutcracker?

Laugh Point____/1

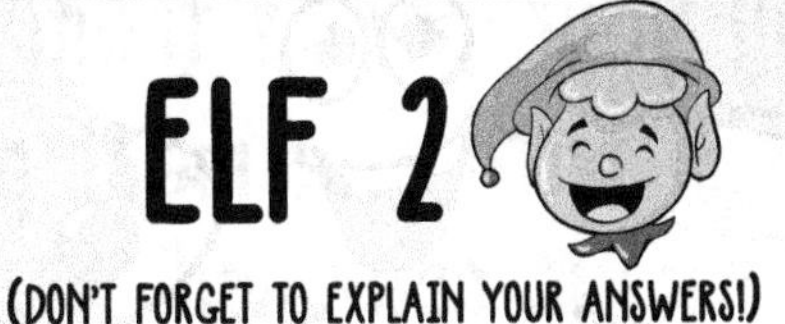

ELF 2

(DON'T FORGET TO EXPLAIN YOUR ANSWERS!)

Would you rather be turned into a snowman OR a gingerbread man?

Laugh Point____/1

Would you rather have socks filled with hot chocolate OR mittens filled with snow?

Laugh Point____/1

Add up all your points from Round 11.
The ELF with the most points
is crowned
The Laugh Master!

ELF 1 ______ /4
ROUND TOTAL

ELF 2 ______ /4
ROUND TOTAL

____

The Laugh Master

Check out our

Visit our Amazon Store at:

other joke books!

www.Amazon.com/author/CrazyCorey

CPSIA information can be obtained
at www.ICGtesting.com
Printed in the USA
BVHW040616021121
620542BV00008B/141